IS YOUR CHILD READY FOR SCHOOL?

FINDING THE BEST GRADE PLACEMENT

Judith Davis Kuhn

Judith D. Kuhn

Published by J. La'Verne Designs

ISBN: 978-0-615-78991-0

Book design by J. La'Verne Designs

Printed in the United States of America

Acknowledgments

Even though I could not possibly tell the stories of every child I have taught during my forty-one years in the classroom, I know each one of those children had an effect on who I am today. It has been a privilege for me to be able to teach young children and at the same time advise parents about the best grade placement for each child. I have been so fortunate to work in a school for the past thirty-six years where the administrators not only allowed me, but also encouraged me, to give my opinion to parents regarding grade placement. I am thankful to every one of those administrators for the trust they placed in me.

I also appreciate my school for awarding me a grant from the Bingham Fund for Leadership in Teaching, which provided the funding for the publication of this book. I am so grateful to my publishers, Jennifer and Vernon Foster, who are also the parents of two of my former kindergarten students, Taylor and Alex. Without their support and patience, I never would have completed this project.
I am very appreciative of my co-workers, my fellow kindergarten teachers, and my wonderful assistant teachers that I have had the privilege of working with on a daily basis during my thirty-five years of teaching kindergarten at Forsyth Country Day School.

I thank Cameron Golden, the mother of one of my kindergarten students, Luca, and a former college professor of English, for the time and energy she put into editing this book for me. I would also like to thank my niece Carol Lovett, a former college instructor of creative writing, who edited part of the book as well. Thank you to all of my family members and friends who encouraged me and gave me their feedback on my work. The photographs of my grandchildren on the front and back cover were taken by Kristin Boone, professional photographer and my kindergarten assistant teacher for five years. Although I am impressed by all of her photography, it is my opinion that her best subjects are my grandchildren.

Introduction

This is a book for parents of young children. The idea for this book grew out of a talk that I have given for many years to parents who are facing a difficult and important decision and find themselves in need of some guidance. My forty-one years of teaching and my love for children fueled a desire to write this book, and I am hoping parents will gain insights from it that will help as they make decisions regarding when their children should start school. Even though I also speak to preschool directors and teachers, the focus here is on concrete examples and advice for parents.

Finding the right time to start school can be one of the most important decisions parents ever make about their children. While parents can often follow their state's cut-off date in determining the best time for their child to start school, sometimes a child needs to wait a year before going to kindergarten or possibly have a second chance at kindergarten before going on to first grade. Parents often fear that if they let their child wait a year, the child will be bored during the second year in that particular grade or in subsequent grades. In my experience, this has not been the case. I have never heard a parent say, "I'm sorry I gave my child some extra time," but I have heard many parents say, "If I had known then what I know now, I would have given my child some extra time."

Individualized academic programs can be provided fairly easily for a student spending a second year in a grade, while trying to help an immature child fit in socially and emotionally can be very difficult for the teacher and the child. Giving a child a "gift of time" can help that child gain self-confidence, reach his or her full potential, and make the difference between being a leader or a follower. Making this decision before a child goes to kindergarten is ideal. If overplacement (being a grade ahead of where one ought to be) is discovered when a child is in the middle grades, it is very difficult to fix the problem—possible, but not easy.

The encouragement and positive responses I have received from parents and former students through the years have let me know that this work to which I have devoted my career does have significance. The stories I tell in this book really happened. Working on this project has given me the opportunity to reconnect with some of my former kindergarten students who are now in their thirties and early forties. I have included selections from our correspondence at the end of the book. Although I have known for years that the extra time made a big difference in their lives, I have recently learned that some of them are now applying this approach as they make decisions about when their own children should start school. Knowing this lets me see that my goal as a teacher to positively impact the lives of my students has been realized.

Making a Decision

Educators and parents are often puzzled by students who are obviously very bright yet do not work up to their full potential. When I hear about an underachieving student, the first question I ask is, “When is this child’s birthday?” I have spent the last thirty-five years of my teaching career looking closely at the relationship between a child’s birthday and school success. In my opinion, many students start school too early and are a grade ahead of where they really should be. The difference between loving school or hating school can as simple as making sure each child is in the right grade.

Determining when a child should start school is one of the most important decisions parents will ever make about their child. Unfortunately, most parents do not even realize there is a decision to be made and simply use their state’s cut-off date as a guide. However, the state’s cut-off date is often not the best judge of what placement is best for each child. In fact, state legislatures in various states do not even agree on the right time for a child to enter school. Currently, there are fifteen different cut-off dates in the United States, ranging from July 31 to January 1.[1] The most popular cut-off date is September 1. As of February 2013, there are nineteen states using September 1 as a cut-off date, but that certainly does not mean this particular date is best for every child.

Each child has his or her own rate of development and what might be a good age to start school for one child is not necessarily the same for another. If a child begins school too early, social and/or academic problems can arise in later grades as a result. If the child needs to wait a year before beginning school, the younger the child is when this decision is made, the easier the transition will be for

---

1 Education Commission of the States

everyone. This raises the question: how can parents of

young children make good decisions about when their child should start school?

The first thing parents need to know is that they can make the decision about when their child starts school. They do not have to just abide by the recommendations of the state in which they reside. For example, in North Carolina (where I have taught for the past thirty-eight years), the Board of Education website states the following:

> All public school systems must offer kindergarten, but children are not required to attend. Compulsory attendance applies to children between the ages of seven and sixteen….[2]

Although parents may not let their child begin school any younger than the minimum age for their state, they can allow their child to be older than the minimum by waiting a year before starting school.

In my forty-one years of teaching young children, I have gained a great deal of perspective about determining the correct placement for a child. During my early years in the classroom in particular, my views were changed dramatically by witnessing several specific incidents that caused me to look more closely at the best age for each child to begin school. This book is filled with anecdotes and examples that show why it is so important to give some children the "gift of time."

---

2 The North Carolina Board of Education

A Mother's Intuition

My teaching career began in 1965 at an elementary school in Knoxville, Tennessee. During my second year of teaching there, I learned an important lesson from the mother of two students. I'm sure she did not intend to teach me anything about the developmental placement of children; she was just trying to do what she thought was best for her identical twin sons, Robert and Richard. What I learned from this family eventually changed the focus of my teaching career. Robert was in my class and Richard was in another first grade class in the school. Both boys were cooperative but quiet, and they appeared to be doing fine in first grade. I did not see their lack of participation as a problem. (In fact, having a few quiet children in a roomful of thirty-four first graders can be a blessing.) The twins seldom talked, laughed, or even smiled. Academically, each boy was in the middle of his class.

In early December of that year, their mother asked to have a conference with the principal and the two first grade teachers. We could not imagine why she wanted to talk with us; from our perspective, everything was running smoothly. During the conference we learned that she was considering having the boys not return to school after the December holiday break. Her rationale for this decision was that the boys were just not as excited about school as their sister had been when she was in first grade. Their mother said they never complained about school but they were "dragging out the door on their way to school every morning." Contributing to her decision was the fact that they had been born prematurely and, as a result, she felt they had always been a little slower in their physical and social development. She also told us that the quiet dispositions we witnessed at school were not the same as the outgoing personalities they exhibited at home.

The three of us--the two teachers and the principal did not know how to respond. We had never heard of anyone pulling their children out of school in the middle of the year. We teachers were immediately defensive, as we thought we must not have been making school exciting enough. We felt that we needed to spruce up our program so Robert and Richard would be elated when they talked with their parents about school. At the end of the meeting, we did not advise their mother one way or the other about her decision. We certainly did not encourage her to take them out of school. She had already spoken with their pediatrician about keeping them home and she received no encouragement from him either. Acting on her own intuition, she did it anyway; her sons did not return to school in January. Because there were no public school kindergartens in Tennessee at that time, the twins stayed home for the remainder of that school year.

The following fall, Richard was in my first grade class and Robert was in a different class. These two boys had transformed in amazing ways. They were no longer quiet—they talked, they laughed, they had a bounce in their step. Both of these boys had a confidence that was sorely lacking the year before. It was so obvious that they were comfortable and enjoyed school and were now where they needed to be. Academically, each boy was at the top of his class. When we administered achievement tests to first graders in the spring that year, the twins had near-perfect scores. (Interestingly, Robert and Richard were sitting in separate rooms when they took that test. Each boy missed only one question on the entire test; it was the same question, and they answered it in the very same way—they truly were identical twins!) Although I moved to North Carolina the following summer and lost contact with Robert and Richard, I have no doubt that they continued to be outstanding students. I am convinced that if their parents had not given them that extra year, they would have gone through school as mediocre students with a lack of confidence and, quite possibly, a permanent dislike for school. But because they were given additional time, I feel sure they were able to reach their full potential.

The Results of Overplacement

My experience with the twins made me realize that my own mother had been right about my younger brother Bill. His birthday was November 22. When we were growing up we lived in Tennessee where the cut-off date for school entrance was December 31. This meant Bill would not turn six years old until he had been in first grade for three months. My mother felt Bill was too young to go to school and wanted to wait a year before sending him to first grade. Whenever she talked with family members and friends about the possibility of letting him wait a year before beginning school, they teased her and said she just wanted to keep Bill home with her because he was the youngest of her four children. "You'd better cut those apron strings and let him go," was a comment she heard again and again. Just like Robert and Richard's mother, she received no support from friends and family members, many of whom were educators; but unlike the twins' mother, she caved in to the pressure and, against her better judgment, let Bill start first grade as scheduled. Later in the school year, still concerned, my mother asked Bill's first grade teacher if she thought it would be a good idea for him to spend a second year in the first grade. The teacher said he would be fine in second grade—he was a smart boy, who was a little immature, but he would catch up. She told my mother not to worry about Bill.

Unfortunately, Bill did not "catch up" until his junior year of college. Until the age of nineteen, Bill hated school. I could not understand why. I knew he was as smart as or smarter than I was, and I always loved school. In August, I would count down the days until school started with eager anticipation. I even decided that I was going to be a teacher of young children when I grew up. How could

I love school so much and Bill hate it? As a child, I did not consider that, with my January birthday, I was one of the oldest in my grade whereas Bill was one of the youngest in his.

Because of my close relationship with Bill, I was very aware of everything he experienced. Being almost five years old when Bill was born, I was thrilled to have a baby in our family—I now had my very own, live doll. There was nothing I enjoyed more than taking care of my little brother, carrying him around most of the time when he was an infant and a toddler. To me, he was the smartest, most adorable little boy who ever lived! I paid close attention when he started school, and this happy little boy almost overnight became a very unhappy boy, but only on school days—Bill was very happy on weekends and during summer months. He would make tents out of quilts on the clothesline in our backyard and play outside for hours on end. Bill was never at a loss for ways to entertain himself at home. Just like the twins in my earlier story, he had a charming, outgoing personality away from school. However, when school was in session, he developed numerous headaches and stomachaches. At the time, I thought he was probably faking some of those symptoms, hoping he wouldn't have to go to school; but in retrospect, I doubt very seriously that he was faking anything. He was under a lot of stress. I, as his self-appointed protector, wanted to help him, but I could never figure out how to accomplish that.

Following his high school graduation, Bill was accepted to college on probation. He didn't do very well in his first two years, but at the beginning of his junior year, someone unexpectedly dropped off the debate team and a friend asked Bill if he wanted to join the team. He did, and for the first time, Bill became "turned on" to learning. Bill was a natural at debating. His success in this area led him to become more engaged in all aspects of college. His grades in every subject improved and his grade point average rose considerably. Two years after finishing college, Bill went on to receive a master's degree and he became a university debate coach. He continued his studies further and received a Ph.D. and has been a professor in a graduate school of business and management and the owner of his own consulting company for many years. Indeed, he always was (and is) very smart, just as I had thought. Bill was fortunate to have found an affinity for debating which gave him confidence and the drive to succeed academically. I often wonder what would have happened if our mother had followed her intuition and let Bill wait a year before beginning first grade. Even though his story has a happy ending, he probably would have been spared the struggles he faced during those early school years.

Meeting Resistance

I entered my fourth year of teaching armed with an awareness of developmental placement, but I didn't even have a name for it yet. I just knew that I wanted to share my knowledge with parents in order to keep children from having a school experience similar to my brother's. I had moved to Winston-Salem, North Carolina, and was teaching first grade in a public school. There was a boy named Sam in my class. Every morning for the first few weeks of school, Sam would enter the classroom, put his things at his desk, go into the restroom that was attached to our classroom, and wail for about five minutes. Then he would get himself straightened up and bravely come into the classroom, not having any idea that we all had heard his crying. I would ask him if anything were bothering him or if he wanted to talk about anything. His answer was always the same: "I am fine." I decided to have a conference with Sam's parents and the principal of my school to discuss his unhappiness and to let them know that I had a possible solution to this problem.

As I told his mother (Sam's father was unable to attend the conference) and the principal the stories of my brother and the twins and suggested that maybe Sam needed to wait a year before beginning first grade, the two of them looked at me as if I had lost my mind. Apparently, I had not done a very good job of explaining. The principal told me he had never heard of giving a child an extra year before beginning first grade, which I could understand because until two years earlier, neither had I. Sam's mother told me she had been waiting for him to start school so she could have a full-time job. And now that she had a job, she was not going to give it up in order for Sam to wait a year before beginning school. Just as in Tennessee, there were no public school kindergartens in North Carolina at that time. I told Sam's mother I believed he would probably never do poorly enough in school to have to repeat a grade. In my opinion, he probably would continue to be a mediocre student at best although I felt he had the potential to be so much more than that. But it didn't matter what I said; things were not going to change for Sam. There was a disconnect between my message and what Sam's mother and my principal heard. I had to accept the situation and do whatever I could to help Sam have a good year. He did go on to second grade at the end of that year, but I worried about his future as he progressed through school.

Waiting another year before beginning school is a big decision that could have consequences for other members of the child's family, not just the child. I learned a valuable lesson from Sam's mother—that I always need to try to see the parent's point of view while still being an advocate for the child. Sam's mother may have needed her job in order to put food on the table for her family. In retrospect, talking with Sam's mother gave me insight into how families receive this information and prepared me for the opposition I would encounter from some parents later on in my career.

Because of the resistance I received from Sam's mother and my principal, I temporarily abandoned the idea of helping parents make decisions about when their children should start school. I set aside all that I believed about the developmental placement of children and wondered if I would ever be able to use this information again.

Signs of Stress

I taught first grade two more years, had a baby, and took a six-year hiatus from teaching. My next teaching position was at an independent school as a kindergarten teacher. Billy was four years old when he entered my class. He would turn five in late September. (North Carolina's cut-off date was October 16 at that time.) Billy was the youngest child in the class; some of the boys were a full year older than Billy. It was obvious to me that Billy was trying his best to keep up with the oldest boys in our class. He would watch them and try to do what they were doing. At school, he was definitely a follower and not a leader. It was obvious to me that Billy was a very smart little boy, but kindergarten wasn't as much fun for him as it should have been.

In November, I decided to try for the second time to explain the developmental placement of children – this time, to Billy's parents – even though I still did not possess the correct vocabulary. One important factor that gave me confidence to tell my stories a second time was that I knew I had the full support of Mabel Brandon, the director of my school. When I told Mrs. Brandon about Billy's behaviors and that I would like to recommend that his parents let him spend a second year in kindergarten, she was in total agreement with me. She was basing this support on her many years as a classroom teacher in the middle grades. Year after year she saw that many of the younger children she taught, mainly boys, were at a disadvantage because of their lack of maturity when compared to the older children in their grade.

So, armed with Mrs. Brandon's support, I met with Billy's parents. They listened earnestly as I told them about my experiences with the twins and my brother. I had expected them to be defensive, but instead, I was pleasantly surprised to find that they were very interested in what I had to say. The three of us decided that Billy needed to wait a year before going to first grade. His parents requested that he stay in my class for the remainder of the school year because all his friends in the neighborhood were in school, and Billy would be the only boy at home during the day.

However, by January, his parents and I were seeing some signs of stress in Billy, both in school and at home. Billy always wanted to have his shoes tied tighter. I would tie his shoes and before I knew it, he would ask me to tie them again. Nothing about his shoes had changed, but I would untie them and tie them again. Billy also began frequenting the restroom. The day I realized he was actually urinating every fifteen minutes, I called his parents and recommended that they take him out of school immediately and re-enroll him in kindergarten the following year. They followed my advice. At home, Billy had been exhibiting these same behaviors, but his parents did not realize they were signs of stress and overplacement in school. As soon as Billy was no longer a kindergarten student, he immediately stopped asking his parents to tie his shoes tighter, and his trips to the bathroom gradually became less frequent. Trying to keep up with those older boys apparently had created too much stress for Billy.

During Billy's second year in my kindergarten class, he was a very different little boy. Although I had witnessed a huge change in the twins from one year to the next, I still was not prepared for the changes in Billy. It was apparent that he now loved school. He was comfortable with everything that was happening in our classroom. Billy interacted well with his peers and was not the least bit concerned about anybody's age. He had an adult-like sense of humor that had not even surfaced the year before. He was on top of the world! Billy stayed at my school through the eighth grade and did extremely well, both socially and academically, during all of those years. After the eighth grade, Billy left our school to attend a public high school where he went from being part of a class of 40 to a class of 1000.

I had no contact with Billy or his parents until one day during his senior year of high school when Billy's mother telephoned me. The family had just received a letter from the University of North Carolina at Chapel Hill informing Billy that he had been awarded a Morehead Scholarship, one of the most prestigious college scholarships granted in the state of North Carolina. His mother said she and Billy's father immediately thought back to his experiences in kindergarten when they read the letter from UNC. She said they felt very strongly that if Billy had not been given that second year of kindergarten, he would not even have been considered for this honor. The following Sunday afternoon I visited Billy and his parents. I took him a present—Robert Fulgham's book, *All I Really Need to Know I Learned in Kindergarten.* During that visit, I learned some things about Billy's high school years: he was valedictorian of his class, president of the National Honor Society, president of the French Club, goalie for the varsity boys' soccer team, and captain of the varsity boys' basketball team. He was definitely a well-rounded student. I was so proud to have been the teacher of such an accomplished young man, and I took special pride in knowing the part I had played in his parents' decision to allow Billy to mature at his own pace.

There was one question I wanted to be sure to ask on that Sunday afternoon. After Billy left the room,

I asked his parents if they thought Billy might have been a mediocre student had he not been given that additional year to mature. His father said, "Oh, I think that's true, but that's not all—I think he would have been a stressed-out, mediocre student." Billy's mother mentioned one concern she and Billy's father had when making their decision thirteen years before: Billy's reaction to his friends when they would surely ask him why he was in kindergarten for a second time. Peer pressure and a fear of being teased is understandably a large concern of most parents when making a decision regarding their child's education. Billy's parents discovered there was no need to worry; his friends never even mentioned it.[3]

3 Refer to Billy's remarks as an adult (and those of his mother) in the Correspondence section at the end of the book.

Developmental Screening

During that first year of teaching kindergarten, I learned from a fellow teacher that the Gesell Institute in New Haven, Connecticut[4] had developed a screening tool to help determine a child's developmental age—the age at which a child is behaving. Although I had already learned by osmosis and from my previous years of teaching experience what developmental placement was, I was thrilled to discover an assessment I could administer to help determine developmental age. This sounded like exactly what I needed to enhance my own understanding and allow me to do a better job of explaining to parents the

---

4 "The Gesell Institute's namesake, Arnold Gesell, PhD, MD, began his groundbreaking work in the early 20th century. He developed a set of norms illustrating sequential and predictable patterns of growth and development, used as the basis of the Gesell Developmental Observation.

Dr. Gesell was the first director of the Yale University Clinic now known as the

Yale Child Study Center, as well as the nation's first school psychologist. He was also a founding member of the National Association for Nursing and Education, now known as the National Association for the Education of Young Children (NAEYC).

Following Dr. Gesell's retirement from Yale in 1950, associates Dr. Louise Bates Ames and Dr. Frances Ilg opened the Gesell Institute in New Haven, Connecticut, to continue his life's work. Since that time, the Institute has offered a variety of medical and educational programs and services to promote the healthy development of children and adults worldwide.

Today, the work of the Institute is focused on educating and supporting teachers and parents in order to ensure the future success of all children, in the United States and abroad."

advantages of beginning school at one time over another. A one-week training session was being offered during the following summer at the Broyhill Continuing Education Center of Appalachian State University in Boone, North Carolina; teachers, guidance counselors, and school administrators were invited to attend. Even though I had learned about Dr. Arnold Gesell's work at Yale University in my college child psychology classes, this was the first time I had heard of his assessment, which was published by the Gesell Institute.

The director of my school, Mrs. Brandon, and I attended the week-long training session at Appalachian. It was an unforgettable experience for me. Leading this week of classes was Clyde Gillespie, who was at that time the chief clinical examiner at the Gesell Institute. Not only did I learn the details of the Gesell assessment and how to administer it, but I also heard about the studies that had been done by Dr. Gesell at Yale on 10,000 children and the behaviors that are typical for various stages of development were reviewed. I soaked up every word. Everything Clyde Gillespie said gave credence to what I believed so strongly. This was what I had been hoping to hear for twelve years. Here was the vocabulary I needed. I couldn't wait to get back to the classroom and begin using what I had learned. At the end of the week of classes, I became certified to administer the Gesell School Readiness Test.[5] When school started in the fall, I began to administer Gesells just for practice to all of my kindergarten children. In the spring, with Mrs. Brandon's encouragement, I administered Gesells as a part of our admission process to help determine if children were developmentally ready for kindergarten.

---

5 The latest revision of the test was done in 2010 and is now called The Gesell Developmental Observation-Revised (GDO-R).

Early Reading

John was one of my students during Billy's second year in my kindergarten class, and he was the first student to whom I administered a Gesell School Readiness Test. I would never have dreamed John was not ready for kindergarten, even though he had a September birthday, because John already knew how to read. Nobody taught him; he just began reading at three years of age. When I met him, he was four and could read so well that his parents hid *Time Magazine* and the local newspaper from him at home; they didn't want John to read articles that might confuse or upset him.

I was surprised when during the first two days of school, John acted aggressively toward the other children in our class. I naively assumed he would be mature for his age because he was reading so well. John hit, kicked, bit, scratched, and pinched every child in the class. I spent a lot of time those two days having private talks with John about how to treat other people. At the end of the second day, with his parents' permission, I telephoned his most recent preschool teacher to ask whether John had behaved this way at school the year before. She said that John had not gotten along well with the children in his preschool class either, and that she thought John believed the children didn't like him. When I asked if they did like him, she responded, "No, not really." In addition to the aggressive behavior toward his classmates, John did things to get their attention, which always backfired on him. The teachers had to watch him carefully. When they gave him glue, he would try to eat it; when they gave him scissors, he would try to cut his hair—just for attention. The only time they could count on John to behave himself was when he was reading. He would choose a book from the bookshelves, lie down on the pillows, and read for long periods of time. I asked his preschool teacher if the children knew he was reading and she said they did not. They thought he was just looking at the pictures like they did. This conversation was very enlightening for me and made me realize I had an important job to do immediately: I needed to find a way for John to feel that the children liked him or this aggressive behavior might continue all year. I had an idea.

If John could be our first "Most Important Person" of the year, maybe his aggressive behaviors toward his classmates would stop. Every year that I taught kindergarten, each child in my classroom had a turn being the Most Important Person for a week. The highlight of the week for that child occurred on Wednesday when the child would sit on the floor in the middle of a circle and listen as each classmate told one thing about the Most Important Person that he or she liked. My assistant teacher and I wrote down what everyone said, and then we would make a chart for the child to take home at the end of the week. The way you became the Most Important Person was by having your name randomly drawn out of a small basket. Even though I usually left the name that was drawn to chance, this was an emergency. I removed the names from the basket and placed twenty pieces of folded paper inside with "John" written on each one. I had two reasons for doing this: John needed to hear his classmates tell him what they liked about him so he could relax and be more comfortable; and if I didn't make him the Most Important Person right away, his classmates might not be able to think of anything nice to say about him. I felt that I needed to try to avoid this possible reaction to John's aggressive acts toward them.

After John's name was drawn out of the basket, I reminded him several times that the children would be watching him closely so they could think of something nice to say about him. On Wednesday of that week, the children did say nice things about John. He was obviously impressed as he listened intently, but instead of smiling (which was the usual reaction), John had a serious look on his face. I wondered why. I later learned that with his phenomenal memory, he was memorizing word-for-word what each child was saying about him. He repeated every word to his mother in the car on the way home that day. John's behavior improved tremendously after that week; my plan had worked. However, in many ways, he still seemed younger than his classmates. He avoided math activities and all paper and pencil activities, and he would roll on the floor laughing about things nobody else thought were funny. These were signs of immaturity and they were a stark contrast to his reading ability.

In October, John had just turned five when I administered the Gesell School Readiness Test to him. Even though this was my first Gesell and I was concerned about my ability to score it correctly, it was obvious that John's performance showed he had the social and emotional maturity of a much younger child. I was surprised by this revelation, just as I had been caught off guard by his aggressive behaviors those first two days of school. If I had scored the assessment correctly, the mystery of why John had not gotten along with the children his age in preschool would be solved. When I shared the results of this evaluation with John's parents, I prefaced my remarks with these words: "This is my first Gesell. I don't know if I have scored it correctly, but if I have, John needs to spend another year in kindergarten." His parents were shocked—they knew their child was academically gifted. After much reading, discussion, and thought, they decided to go along with my recommendation. I was pleased when John's parents requested that he be placed in my class again, because the following year, I had the privilege of witnessing my third developmental placement miracle. That year, he got along well with every child in the class. He no longer avoided math or paper and pencil activities. We did give him an individualized reading program during his second year of kindergarten, which enabled him to continue developing his reading skills beyond those of his classmates. In other areas, he learned at the same pace as the rest of the class. He now had many friends and was well liked by all of his classmates. To my knowledge, John was never again aggressive toward another child during his entire school experience.

Creating an individualized academic program like we did for John can be very important to ensure the success of a child who is immature, yet whose academic skills are advanced. Understandably, some parents fear that if they let their child wait a year, the child will be bored and will not be academically challenged the second year in the same grade. But, tailoring an individualized program for children like John is so much easier—for the teacher as well as the student—than trying to help a child fit in with classmates when the child is socially and emotionally young for that particular grade.

When John was in the fourth grade, he and his parents moved to Nashville, Tennessee. I did not hear from John again until the summer after his freshman year of college, when he stopped by my classroom one day in June on his way to a relative's high school graduation. John was surprised that I recognized him and that I was able to call him by his first and last name. His exact words were, "I can't believe you would remember me after all of these years." I told him I could never forget him—that his was one of my best developmental placement stories. He responded that his parents had always said that having him spend a second year in kindergarten was the best decision they ever made about him. I told John I was glad to hear that because I was new at helping parents make decisions about grade placement at the time. John and I walked from my classroom to the car where his parents and his grandmother were waiting for him. I learned that John had just completed his freshman year at the University of Notre Dame on a full ROTC scholarship. Much to John's embarrassment, his father told me that John had been honored at his high school graduation as the athlete with the highest academic average. Having the highest academic average did not surprise me at all, but the athlete part of that statement amazed me. I never thought John would become an athlete—a rocket scientist perhaps, but not an athlete. In fact, during his junior and senior years he went to six consecutive state finals in three different sports: cross country, swimming, and track. Later, he was in the running for Athlete of the Decade from his high school. John's mother gave me her phone number and said, "If parents ever have any doubt about whether or not to give their child more time, just tell them to call me." This affirmation made me even more determined to continue my mission of helping parents make good decisions about when their children should begin school—one child at a time.

Many well-meaning educators might have said the reason John acted aggressively in preschool and at the beginning of his first year of kindergarten was that he was bored and was not being academically challenged enough. They might have placed him in a higher grade according to his reading level. In my opinion, that approach would have been a huge mistake for John. It is my belief that had John not spent a second year in kindergarten, he would have become a social misfit. I think teachers would have ended up separating him from his classmates to do what he did best—read. He may have been given extra book reports and projects to work on to keep him busy and out of trouble. If this had happened, he might never have developed his social skills or athletic abilities. Had he not spent a second year in kindergarten, I believe John would not have been able to develop into the well-rounded individual he obviously became.[6]

---

6 Refer to John's letter as a college student in the Correspondence section at the end of the book.

One School's Guidelines

The number of children who are overplaced in school (a grade ahead of where they would be best suited by using their maturity level as a guide) varies from state to state, depending on a particular state's cut-off date. The standard we use at my current school is for children to be five years old developmentally by September 1 when entering kindergarten. This means that regardless of their actual ages, we want to see them score as five years old on the Gesell Developmental Observation. This is not our only guide. We also have preschool teachers and parents answer questions about the child on observation forms. Most boys who are given the Gesell in our school test as six months younger developmentally than their actual ages, while most girls' chronological age and developmental age are the same. Using this as a guide, a boy would ideally need to be chronologically five and a half by September 1 when entering kindergarten, making March 1 a good cut-off date for boys. However, I like to remind parents that this is not a hard and fast rule and that every child develops at his or her own rate. To be on the safe side, we have found July 1 to be a good cut-off date for girls, even though this is not exactly six months after the boy's ideal cut-off date. July 1 is the date my school uses as its "official" cut-off date, but since we are an independent school, we can and do make exceptions.

In my thirty-five years of helping parents decide when their child is ready to begin school, it has been my experience that parents are always correct if either the mother or the father thinks the child needs to be given more time. However, the opposite of that is not true—just because parents think their child is ready doesn't necessarily make it so. I believe the reason for this is that it is difficult for parents to be objective about their own child. When parents do recognize the need for their child to wait a year with no outside recommendations, it is generally because the social and emotional immaturity of their child is quite evident or because of previous family experiences. Hindsight is a great teacher in this regard. As I said in the Introduction of this book, many parents say to me, "If I had known then what I know now, I would have given my child some extra time." But never, not even once, has a parent said to me, "I'm sorry I gave my child some extra time." Leonard Sax, M.D., Ph.D., addressed school readiness in his book *Boys Adrift*:

> Doing something earlier doesn't necessarily mean that you will do it any better. In fact, it may mean that you do it less well in the long run. (22)

A Father's Reaction

When I make the recommendation for a child to be given additional time to parents during conferences, the reaction to my advice varies. While responses are usually very positive, sometimes there are serious reservations. In one particular conference, I told the parents that their seven-year-old son, a second-grade applicant to our school with a September birthday, needed to be in first grade rather than second. His mother asked me a lot of questions about developmental placement, while his father just sat there quietly listening. In my experience, when a parent is silent during a conference, it is often an indication of resistance to my recommendations. I assume then that I need to work harder to convince that particular parent. In this case, I turned to the father and asked if he had any questions for me. He replied, "No, I have just been sitting here thinking about what happened to me when I was in school." I asked him to explain. He said his parents were convinced that he should start first grade when he was only five years old, because he was "so smart."

When he was in fourth grade, he wasn't enjoying school, and his parents met with the principal and his fourth grade teacher. It was decided that he just wasn't being challenged enough and that he needed to skip a grade, which then placed him two years ahead of where he should have been. His grades were okay but not great, and his parents and teachers were always saying, "You're not applying yourself," or "You could do so much better if you would just try harder." In his own mind, he was trying his best, but he could never meet the expectations of his parents and teachers. Even though everyone thought he was smart, he certainly didn't feel very smart. After graduating from high school at sixteen, it took him eight years to get his college degree. He then went into the U. S. Army for four years, and it was during that four-year period that he finally, as he said, "came into his own." He was accepted to Harvard Business School and received his Ph. D. in three years. For the first time in his life, he thought maybe he was smart after all. This father definitely had no qualms about allowing his son to be given some more time at this early stage. He would never want his child to repeat his own miserable experience. I learned from this father that I should never assume that I know what parents are thinking, and I need to be sure to ask questions to give them the opportunity to express their feelings.

A Child's View

Most parents are concerned about the reaction of their child to hearing the news that he or she will be spending a second year in a particular grade. I have heard some really humorous reactions through the years. Malay's story is a good example of how you can never assume you know what a child is thinking.

Malay had a December birthday, so he was almost six when he started kindergarten. There was no way he would be spending a second year in kindergarten. He was not young for his grade, and he had done well both socially and academically all year long. Just before the end of the school year, Malay's mother was a few minutes late picking him up from school one day. As Malay and I sat on a bench in front of the school waiting for her, he looked up at me and stated, "Mrs. Kuhn, I'm going to be in kindergarten again next year." With an element of surprise in my voice, I replied, "You are?" "Yes, I told my mother last night that I'm going to be in kindergarten next year and you are going to be my teacher again." I asked him what his mother had said. "We'll see," was her reply. I told Malay that in a couple of weeks I would have private talks with each one of the children in my class, and at that time I would let each of them know if they would be going on to first grade or spending another year in kindergarten. I'll never forget Malay's response: "Oh, I get it now! If we be real good, we get to be in kindergarten two years!" He apparently thought being given an extra year was an honor. Of course, when I did have the private talk with him, I told him he would be going to first grade. He was disappointed, but only momentarily. When I mentioned this conversation to his mother, we agreed that we had no idea why Malay was thinking this way—maybe he just wanted to stick with something familiar.

I have found for younger children there is no stigma attached to waiting a year before going to kindergarten or first grade. As mentioned before, the younger the child is when this decision is made, the easier the transition will be for everyone. One thing I tried not to do in my classroom was make comments that began with, "Next year when you're in first grade…." I never wanted to have to backtrack during my private talk with a child who would be spending another year in kindergarten. I would then have had to say, "When I said, 'Next year, when you're in first grade….' I was talking to all of the other children except you." Needing to say this could have undermined the trust children placed in me as their teacher. I always worked hard to build a trusting relationship with my students, and I never would have wanted to do anything that would violate that trust. Instead, I might say from time to time, "When you're in first grade…."

Breaking the News

When I had the individual talk with my students, it was always on the next-to-the-last day of school. I told the children they could not talk about our private conversation at school—only at home. By the time I met with them, I already knew their parents were in total agreement with my recommendation. The reason I asked the children not to talk about our conversation at school was to avoid any innocent comments by classmates that could have caused the child to be uncomfortable. One year a mother asked me to telephone her as soon as I told her son he would be spending a second year in kindergarten. She just knew he would fall apart and she would need to come to school to pick him up early that day. When I made that phone call, I was able to tell her that her son was so excited about getting to spend a second year in kindergarten that he was dancing around the room, all smiles, begging me to let him tell his classmates. His mother thought this must be an act he was putting on just for me—that he was hiding his true feelings. Two months into the summer, I called her to ask how her son was feeling about being in kindergarten again. She said, "If it were just an act, then he is still acting." She said he was telling everyone he knew that he was going to be in kindergarten again. He was so excited!

If a young child does need to be given some additional time, I have found that it is better to let the school and/or teacher accept the responsibility for that decision rather than the parents, even though the parents' opinions are a major part of the decision making process. I remember one set of parents who did not agree with me when I suggested being the person who broke the news to their son Michael that he would be spending another year in kindergarten. They thought Michael would be more receptive to the idea if they told him it was their decision. Of course, I conceded. Michael was their son, after all. They told him they had made a mistake by letting him start school too soon, and now he needed to spend another year in kindergarten because of their error. He was mad at them for a while, but as soon as school started in the fall, it didn't take long for Michael to realize he was in the right place, so he wasn't mad anymore. Kindergarten was easier and so much more fun for him that second time around.

Different guidelines may need to be followed when an older child is receiving the news of spending a second year in a grade. One approach can be to let the child become a part of the decision making process. If the child is feeling academic or social stress, often it can be a relief to know there is a possibility of having a second chance to master that grade. Jim Grant, author of more than twenty books and founder of the company Staff Development for Educators, wrote on this subject in his book, *Struggling Learners: Below Grade or Wrong Grade?*:

> A student does not—repeat not—have to feel badly[sic] about taking an additional year to complete a grade. In fact, students can feel very good about having this opportunity—and very good about themselves once the opportunity arrives.
>
> What makes the difference in how students feel about an additional year of learning and growing time? Obviously, the actual experience has a lot to do with it, but so does the way in which it is presented.
>
> In talking with a student about taking an additional year to complete a grade, it is imperative to include three key elements in the conversation, if you want the student to have the positive attitude that will help create academic success.

> 1. Make it abundantly clear to the student that the grown-ups in the student's life made a mistake when they unknowingly allowed a young child to be placed in the wrong grade or program—one for which he or she was not ready.
>
> 2. Enlist the student's aid in correcting this unfortunate mistake and helping to set things right.
>
> 3. Make it clear that there is now agreement among the most important grown-ups (parents, teacher, and principal) that an additional year of learning and growing time is in the student's best interest. And make sure the student understands that he or she has the whole-hearted support of all these adults. (127-128)

When I speak privately with a kindergarten child letting him know about the fact that he will be getting a second chance at kindergarten, my goals are to make the conversation appropriate for his age and to help the child get on board with the plan. I usually talk about how some things have been easy and some things have been hard and that I want everything to be easier next year. I might mention how much this child likes to play with the blocks and cars and trucks and that I think it's important for him to be able to have time to play at school again the following year. Depending on the child's birthdate, I might say something about his being one of the youngest children in the class and I think it would be better if he were one of the oldest children in the class. At this point, I tell him that he and his parents get to decide which kindergarten teacher he will have next year. I then encourage the child to choose another kindergarten teacher, so he will have a different experience the following year. However, if the child and his parents choose to be in my class again, the school will accept their decision. This formula has worked well during the past thirty-five years; children have always had a positive reaction to the news when it has been presented in this fashion.

A Reluctant Father

Several years ago, the father of one of my kindergarten students had a very difficult time accepting my recommendation that his son Quinlan spend an extra year in kindergarten. Quinlan's mother was in agreement with the recommendation; his father was not. He said he would go along with the decision, but he had serious doubts. During Quinlan's second year in my class, his father agreed that his son was having a good year, but he still wasn't convinced that it had been the right decision. When their son was in second grade, Quinlan's mother walked into my office and told me I needed to read Malcolm Gladwell's book, *Outliers: the Story of Success*. She said her husband had just read the book, and now he finally understood why it was important for their son to be one of the oldest children in his class rather than one of the youngest. I bought a copy of the book that very week to find out what Gladwell said that made such a difference in this father's understanding of developmental placement.

The part that undoubtedly influenced Quinlan's father the most was Gladwell's discussion of Roger Barnsley's research into the concept of relative age. Barnsley became interested in investigating the connection between birthdates and success when he and his wife attended a Junior Hockey League game in Canada. His wife was looking at the roster of players and noticed that the vast majority of the players had January, February, or March birthdates. When they returned home, Barnsley looked up the birthdates of as many professional hockey players as he could find:

> The more he looked, the more Barnsley came to believe that what he was seeing was not a chance occurrence but

> an iron law of Canadian hockey: in any elite group of Hockey players—the very best of the best—40 percent of the players will have been born between January and March, 30 percent between April and June, 20 percent between July and September, and 10 percent between October and December. (22-23)
>
> Barnsley argues that these kinds of skewed age distributions exist whenever three things happen: selection, streaming, and differentiated experience. If you make a decision about who is good and who is not good at an early age; if you separate the "talented" from the "untalented"; and if you provide the "talented" with a superior experience, then you're going to end up giving a huge advantage to that small group of people born closest to the cutoff date. (25)

Gladwell goes on to say that Major League Baseball in the United States and European soccer are both organized similarly to hockey in Canada. When you look at a roster of players, you will see that every year those whose birthdays are just past the cut-off date are usually the ones chosen for the teams. He related athletic success to grade placement in this way:

> Hockey and soccer are just games, of course, involving a select few. But these exact same biases also show up in areas of much more consequence, like education. Parents with a child born at the end of the calendar year often think about holding their child back before the start of kindergarten: it's hard for a five-year-old to keep up with a child born many months earlier. But most parents, one suspects, think that whatever disadvantage a younger child faces in kindergarten eventually goes away.
> But it doesn't. It's just like hockey. The small initial advantage that the child born in the early part of the year has over the child born at the end of the year persists.

> It locks children into patterns of achievement and underachievement, encouragement and discouragement, that stretch on and on for years. (27-28)

This research into sports and the correlation to birthdays and cut-off dates spoke to Quinlan's father. Since then, I have recommended *Outliers* to parents when I give my talks about school readiness and developmental placement. One never knows when there might be another reluctant parent in the audience who would benefit from the information found in Gladwell's book.[7]

---

7 Refer to Quinlan's father's remarks in the Correspondence section at the end of the book.

The Shy Child

What are some of the signs that can alert parents and teachers to the fact that a child might be overplaced in school? One of the most obvious signs of stress is aggressive behavior. John, the kindergarten student who acted aggressively toward his classmates the first two days of school, is a perfect example. Another sign can be the opposite of that—a child who exhibits extremely quiet, shy behavior.

Page is a good example of a very shy child whom I had in my kindergarten class one year. She frequently brought things to school for Show and Tell, but she could not look at the children when it was her turn to tell about what she brought. She would hold the object in front of her and look at the wall behind her as she spoke. Her younger sister was very outgoing and when Page wasn't in school, she would let her sister do all the talking for both of them. Page's parents were the ones who brought up the question of her readiness; they wondered if it would help her to spend a second year in kindergarten before going on to first grade. Would she be less shy and have more self-confidence? I had not even considered this possibility because Page's birthday was in April. For a girl, she was not that young. Her parents decided to try letting her repeat kindergarten. They wanted her to be in my class again because they were worried it might take a while for her to warm up to a new teacher. We decided if Page were still just as shy that second year, we would move her to first grade within the first month of school, because we would know the shyness was a personality trait as opposed to being an indication of her maturity level. However, I was truly amazed at the difference in Page's personality that second year in kindergarten.

It was apparent to me during the first few days of school that she was no longer quiet and shy. She was not boisterous, either, but she was definitely not shy. One day when two classmates were trying to figure out how to play a board game, Page jumped right in and said, "I'll show you how to play that game." She smiled and talked and thoroughly enjoyed every activity during that second year. She looked directly at her classmates when it was her turn for Show and Tell. Giving her that extra time to mature was definitely the right thing to do. Page went on to hold leadership positions during high school and college. A few years ago, I ran into Page at a bridal shower for a mutual friend. As we conversed, Page told me that she remembered how she felt that first year of kindergarten and how much happier she was during her second year. Page thanked me for giving her the opportunity to mature at a comfortable pace rather than being pushed ahead before she was ready. I told her it was her parents who suggested that she be given a second chance at kindergarten. She said, "Well, they give you all of the credit." Not only did Page's parents provide an opportunity for their daughter to succeed, they taught me even more about how to recognize a lack of readiness for school. I learned that shyness isn't always a personality trait. It can be a significant indicator of a lack of maturity.[8]

Along with shyness, other behaviors that may be exhibited by children who are overplaced are stomachaches, headaches, bed-wetting, chewing on fingers, and complaints about school. When determining a child's maturity level, one thing that is not an indicator is the height of the child. Tall children are not necessarily mature, and short children are not always immature. Unfortunately,

---

8 Refer to Page's remarks as an adult (and those of her mother) in the Correspondence section at the end of the book.

society tends to expect more from tall children and less from short children. Parents and teachers may find themselves saying, "You're too big to be doing that" to a child who is tall for his or her age. Parents and teachers should try not to allow a child's size to influence their ideas about that child's readiness. In my experience, taking a holistic approach to evaluating the child is the only way to guarantee they are placed correctly.

Multiples

Often I am asked my opinion about twins (or triplets)—what should a family do if one is developmentally young and the other one is not? Should they be in different grades in school? My answer is always the same—they should not be in separate grades unless there is a huge maturity gap. It is my opinion that parents should place both twins in the grade that is appropriate for the twin who is younger developmentally. The more mature twin will not suffer by being one of the oldest children in the grade, but the one who is pushed ahead could be miserable for many years as a result of overplacement.

Several years ago, a few days after school started, the parents of a set of twins, a girl and a boy with summer birthdays, applied for their children to be in our first grade. At that time, the twins, Mary and Jason, were enrolled in first grade in another school, and already it had not been a good experience for them, especially for Jason. He told his parents he did not want to go to school. One morning they were late for school because the family had to spend time searching for Jason's clothes and shoes—the ones his mother had set out for him the night before. They later discovered that he had hidden his clothes and shoes hoping they would not be found and he would then be allowed to stay home from school. The parents decided they needed to look into the possibility of changing schools, so they brought the twins to my school. I administered the Gesell assessment to both of them as part of our admission process. Their scores showed that, according to their developmental ages, one twin definitely needed to be in kindergarten but the other one could have gone to either first grade or kindergarten. My advice to their parents was to place both of them in kindergarten. I believed they should not be in separate grades. During that second year in kindergarten, both Jason and Mary loved school. They were outstanding students. Jason never hid his clothes and shoes again. Kindergarten was where they needed to be. Mary is now a high school teacher and Jason is an architect. Their parents say giving them that extra time is the best thing they ever did for them.[9]

---

9 Refer to remarks by Jason and Mary as adults in the Correspondence section at the end of the book.

Questioning the Test Results

From time to time, parents do challenge the scores on their child's evaluation. As I mentioned, it is not easy for some parents to be objective about their own child, and sometimes they try to rationalize a younger score. When I first began administering the Gesell, there were several cases where parents questioned the results. One Gesell assessment placed a young girl in pre-kindergarten rather than in kindergarten, where her parents wanted her to be. When they saw the scores, her parents told me they had hosted a dinner party in their home the night before her scheduled appointment. They put their daughter to bed and assumed she had gone to sleep. Much later, they saw her at the top of the stairs, looking through the rails, watching and listening. She had stayed up long past her usual bedtime. They asked if we would be willing to administer another evaluation on a day she was well rested to see if that would make a difference, which was not our usual practice. We usually wait at least six months before administering the Gesell a second time, but to appease these parents, we gave another Gesell to this child right away. Her scores rose a bit, so we decided to let her try kindergarten, with the understanding that she might need to spend a second year in kindergarten rather than go on to first grade. That is exactly what happened. The child's kindergarten teacher could tell within the first few months of school that she would need to be given some more time before going on to first grade. The original evaluation had, indeed, been accurate.

I am often asked if there is a better time of the year for a child to be given the Gesell Developmental Observation. Although it can be administered anytime during the year, my preference is to evaluate children in January, February, or March. A child who is being considered for kindergarten in the fall would need to be at least four and a half developmentally in February in order to be five years old developmentally by September 1. This assumes the child will advance six months developmentally in six months' time, which is usually the case. When we make a recommendation for placement, we do consider the month the Gesell was given. Following this schedule gives no advantage or disadvantage in giving the Gesell at one time over another.

Correspondence from Former Students and Parents

As I was writing this book, I decided to reach out to some of the people I mention in my stories to find out how they feel now about the decisions that were made years ago. It was not possible for me to get in touch with all of them, but I have included responses from several former students and their parents.

Billy

I do believe that the shift from being one of the youngest boys in my class to being one of the oldest made a hugely positive difference for me as I moved through school. It couldn't have hurt academically, but more importantly I think it helped a great deal socially – and, related, athletically. It's hard to say for sure, but I do think I would have been significantly more stressed had I stayed "on track" with the state cut-off date, trying to keep up with the older boys.

As for my thinking about my own boys, yes, it has been affected by my own experience. The school our boys attend (or will attend) uses a June 1 cut-off date for first grade, but a later date for kindergarten. Using those guidelines, my eldest will have two years of kindergarten and will be one of the oldest in his class – which I think will be very good for him. Moreover, the school de-emphasizes the academic rat race that seems to be infiltrating the grade school years at so many schools. They let the kids be kids for a while, which also resonates with my "gift of time" experience. Harvard can wait. ;-)

At the end of the day, here's what's telling: I feel

compelled to thank you. Thank you for noticing what was happening with me. Thank you for talking with my parents those many years ago (even as you struggled finding the right words for explaining developmental placement). Thank you for recommending that I pull out of school early when I was showing such signs of stress. Now that I know more of your own story and how you came to your understanding of developmental placement, I appreciate you and the gift of you that much more. I feel truly blessed that you were there for that stressed out little boy. The adult 'me' sends you a deep and heartfelt thanks. So, yes, though I'm not sure I can pinpoint or quantify it, I suppose I do feel like it's made a great deal of difference in the quality of my life.

Billy's Mother

As parents, we had absolutely NO regrets of how this situation was handled. In fact, we were very happy telling other parents that we would do the same thing again in a heartbeat. I feel strongly that as a parent you need to be very observant of changes (no matter how subtle or blatant) in your child's behavior as he may be trying to tell you something without being able to express himself verbally.

John (He was a college student when he wrote this letter. I had just sent him the book *All I Really Need to Know I Learned in Kindergarten* by Robert Fulghum.)

Dear Mrs. Kuhn,

Let me begin this letter by expressing an undying gratitude for both the book and its accompanying letter. It really doesn't seem that long since I left your class at FCDS, even though time tells me differently through every perusal of the '79-'81 yearbooks. It's been many years and a set of braces since then, so to finally see you again and to find that you haven't changed much was a pleasure that was altogether comforting. Please forgive the hasty exit—I could have talked for hours, but my 83-year-old grandmother is diabetic and was getting cranky without her lunch (You know how they get.).

On a serious note, though, it is my belief that everyone is born with the same innate talents that either progress or digress while branching into different areas of interest. These are weighed upon by certain factors such as home life, willingness to learn, etc., and can be directly proportional to the level of self-esteem that the child/student has. I would like to thank you for your time through the Gesell Developmental Evaluation program, because through this, I became aware of me as a student as opposed to me as a toddler. By this I mean that your program allowed me to mature at a pace that was comfortable to me—a "becoming civilized," as Fulghum would have put it. I owe a lot of my success in school to my parents, but I know that my success in the actual classrooms that I have darkened had to start somewhere—that "somewhere" being at the very end of the hall of the Lower School at FCDS in your classroom.

I wish you the greatest of successes with your program because with your guidance there will always be a harvest of excellence, an option that is forever renewable at FCDS.

Your Student,
John

Quinlan's Father

There is an immediate parental reaction of disbelief

when a proud parent of a gifted child is asked if they agree that their child should be held in kindergarten. There is little context for a conversation that leads to a simple acceptance of that recommendation, even when it's delivered by a trusted expert. The fact is that most of us relate our child's development to physical and intelligence triggers, such as height-weight scales or reading/math basics, respectively. Quinlan had no issues in these areas. The subtle signals that you keyed in on were off our radar. Following our discussion, I went in search of validation of the idea. There was a full spectrum of opinions. One compelling reference came from the owner of the company for which I work. This colleague and friend supported the idea, as he faced the same dilemma and pursued the same course with his son (another very successful outcome). Then I ran across Malcolm Gladwell's book. I immediately felt ahead of the curve in the understanding of ways in which to support our son's development. The impact on me of Gladwell's concept of "accumulative advantage" was to pose a direct question to us: did we want to put our son in a position to benefit from such an advantage or to have him chasing those who were already realizing this advantage? Your counsel and insights provided us with the mechanism to allow Quinlan to develop within a peer group based on developmental readiness and not an arbitrary calendar date. Quinlan is now thriving at FCDS. As you predicted, he is grouped as "highly academically gifted" among his peers. It started with your advice and my meeting with you. That is a wonderful gift. I thank you.

Page

At thirty-two I look back at my childhood as one of (if not the most) wonderful times in my life. I was so very fortunate to have two loving parents who gave of themselves so generously and took such a strong and active role in making decisions about my education that would shape who I am today. My parents decided to "hold me back" in kindergarten. I don't remember the fact that I was repeating kindergarten as being a defining moment as a child. I can't even remember how my parents or my kindergarten teacher, Ms. Kuhn, told me. I do remember that I enjoyed my second year with Ms. Kuhn much more so than my first year. I know without question that having an extra year to grow, learn from peers, and understand myself better affected my confidence and helped shape a bright future for me.

Along with my parents being proactive and forward-thinkers, my kindergarten teacher, Judith Kuhn, was the one who presented and encouraged the idea of my staying back a year. I feel so very fortunate that as a child I had not only loving parents who were strong enough to make tough decisions about my education but also a revolutionary in a elementary teacher who cared so much to recommend a novel idea at the time and to also be a support system for my parents.

Today I am a working woman living in our nation's capital. I feel so very blessed by the many opportunities that have been afforded to me. I realize that in life some things happen for a reason, but more importantly most things happen when you put your mind to it and work hard to accomplish your goals. I cannot credit my happiness to one specific turn of events; but I believe knowing yourself, understanding where you come from, realizing your strengths and weaknesses, and being able to rise to the occasion are fundamental tenets to my life. I also believe education is key and having a strong foundation in elementary school enabled me with tools for life. I thank my parents and Ms. Kuhn for taking the risk and making the right decision to give me a second year of kindergarten.

Page's Mother

Giving Page an extra year in kindergarten was one of the best decisions my husband and I made for her during her eighteen years under our wings. She was a bright, loving little girl who was shy. Being shy is different from being quiet; it is much more restricting. I think Page's shyness came from being very attached to me and from lacking self-confidence. In 1980 when Page started kindergarten, few parents or teachers realized how crucial it was to consider each child's development before sending him or her to first grade. Without Judith Kuhn's guidance, I wouldn't have considered holding Page back in kindergarten since she wasn't a child who couldn't read, color, cut, or sit still. She simply needed another year to find the confidence to lift the restrictions of shyness. During Page's second year in kindergarten, she blossomed. She made many friends and actually became a role model in the classroom. Page continued to excel academically and socially throughout elementary school, high school, and college.

Today at age thirty-two, Page is still my bright, loving little girl; however, her shyness has been replaced with a confidence that allows her to live every moment to the fullest. She is the Education Director for the White House Fellows program in Washington, DC. This position requires decision-making skills, public speaking skills, social skills, and leadership skills – all of which she and I both attribute to her having a second year in kindergarten. Without the extra year, I believe Page would have become a bright, loving adult, but would she have had the confidence to go after her dreams and grasp every opportunity? I'm afraid not.

Mary (one of the twins)

As for my thoughts on spending a second year in kindergarten, I think it was great for us! I never thought it was a big deal. We were always a little older in each grade and that maturity helped us in lower school all the way through high school. It never bothered me in any way that we repeated kindergarten...it was the best choice for us and we were blessed to have parents and teachers like you looking out for us!

Jason (the other twin)

I never really thought of it as repeating kindergarten. It was important for us to be both physically and academically prepared to enter school. It was also vitally important for us to be together. Clearly, I wasn't ready for the first grade and I know I would never have become a successful student and adult had my twin not been there every step of the way. Thankfully, we had parents who listened to us and would not allow us to start off on the wrong foot. They found the right place for us and we had excellent teachers who created a comfortable learning environment that I believe set us both on the path at that early age that would allow us to realize our career goals as adults.

Conclusion

My goal for writing this book was to encourage and empower parents to be open-minded about the best grade placement for their child. If they can learn from my experiences with students and their parents, then hopefully they will ask teachers and administrators the right questions, understand their child's behaviors, and ultimately make the best decision for their family.

Works Cited

"50-State Analysis." Education Commission of the States. February 28, 2013. <http://ecs.force.com/mbdata/mbquestU?SID=a0i70000004J3c-q&rep=Kq02&Q=Q3195>.

Gladwell, Malcolm. Outliers: The Story of Success. New York: Little, Brown and Company, 2008.

Grant, Jim. Struggling Learners: Below Grade or Wrong Grade? New Jersey: Modern Learning Press, 2002.

"Our History." The Gesell Institute. February 28, 2013. <http://www.gesellinstitute.org/history.html>.

Sax, Leonard. Boys Adrift. New York: Basic Books, 2009.

"School Entry Age." North Carolina State Board of Education. February 28, 2013. <http://stateboard.ncpublicschools.gov/legal-affairs/resources-1/school-entry-age>.